- ACCORDING TO YOUR TASTE
- BASED ON YOUR BROWSING HISTORY
- BASED ON YOUR BROWSING PURCHASE
- BASED ON YOUR HISTORY
- BASED ON YOUR INTEREST IN
- BASED ON YOUR RECENT VISIT
- BASED ON YOUR VIEWING HISTORY
- BECAUSE YOU PURCHASED RECOMMENDED FOR YOU
- COMPANION PRODUCTS
- CUSTOMERS ALSO BOUGHT
- CUSTOMERS ALSO VIEWED
- CUSTOMERS WHO PURCHASED
- ALSO ENJOYED
- FIRST NAME, TRY
- HAVE YOU SEEN THESE YET?
- IF YOU LIKE THIS, TRY THESE
- IF YOU LIKE THIS, YOU'LL LOVE
- INSPIRED BY YOUR BROWSING HISTORY
- INVESTMENT RECOMMENDATION
- JUST FOR YOU
- MAKE IT EXTRA SPECIAL! ADD
- MORE FANCY THINGS
- MORE GREAT ITEMS
- MORE ITEMS LIKE
- MORE LIKE
- NEARBY GROUPS
- OTHERS LIKED THESE SIMILAR ITEMS
- PEOPLE ALSO BOUGHT
- PERSONALIZED PRODUCT RECOMMENDATIONS
- PERSONALIZED RECOMMENDATIONS
- RECOMMENDATION, JUST FOR YOU!
- RECOMMENDATIONS FOR YOU
- RECOMMENDED FOR YOU
- RECOMMENDED VIDEOS FOR YOU
- RELATED ITEMS
- RELATED PRODUCTS
- SIMILAR PRODUCTS
- SPONSORED CONTENT
- SUGGESTED FOR YOU
- SUGGESTED GROUP
- SUGGESTED POST
- THIS CAUGHT YOUR EYE
- YOU MIGHT ALSO LIKE THESE
- TRY FOR FREE
- WE RECOMMEND
- WE SUGGEST THESE ADDITIONAL ACCESSORIES
- YOU MAY ALSO LIKE
- YOU MAY ALSO NEED ONE OF THESE ITEMS
- YOU MAY BE INTERESTED IN
- YOU MAY LIKE
- YOU MIGHT BE INTERESTED IN THESE ITEMS
- YOUR FRIENDS ALSO LIKED
- YOUR RECENT PURCHASES ARE SIMILAR TO
- YOUR TASTE PREFERENCES CREATED THIS ROW

FROM SURVEILLANCE CAPITALISM TO GLITCH CAPITALISM

01 SOUSVEILLANCE OF BIG TECH COMPANIES USING THEIR OWN TOOLS
-> DISNOVATION.ORG

02 EXCESSIVE BIG-DATA MINING AS A RIPOSTE STRATEGY
-> ALESSANDRO LUDOVICO

03 FROM SURVEILLANCE CAPITALISM TO GLITCH CAPITALISM
-> AN INTERVIEW WITH DISNOVATION.ORG BY INGA SEIDLER (EXCERPT)

04 PROFILING THE PROFILERS
-> PROTOTYPES & EXHIBITION VIEWS

Google

why we should own our data

ALL IMAGES VIDEOS NEWS MAPS

Did you mean: why we should own *your* data

1
PROFILING
THE PROFILERS

SOUSVEILLANCE
OF BIG TECH
COMPANIES
USING THEIR
OWN TOOLS

DISNOVATION.ORG

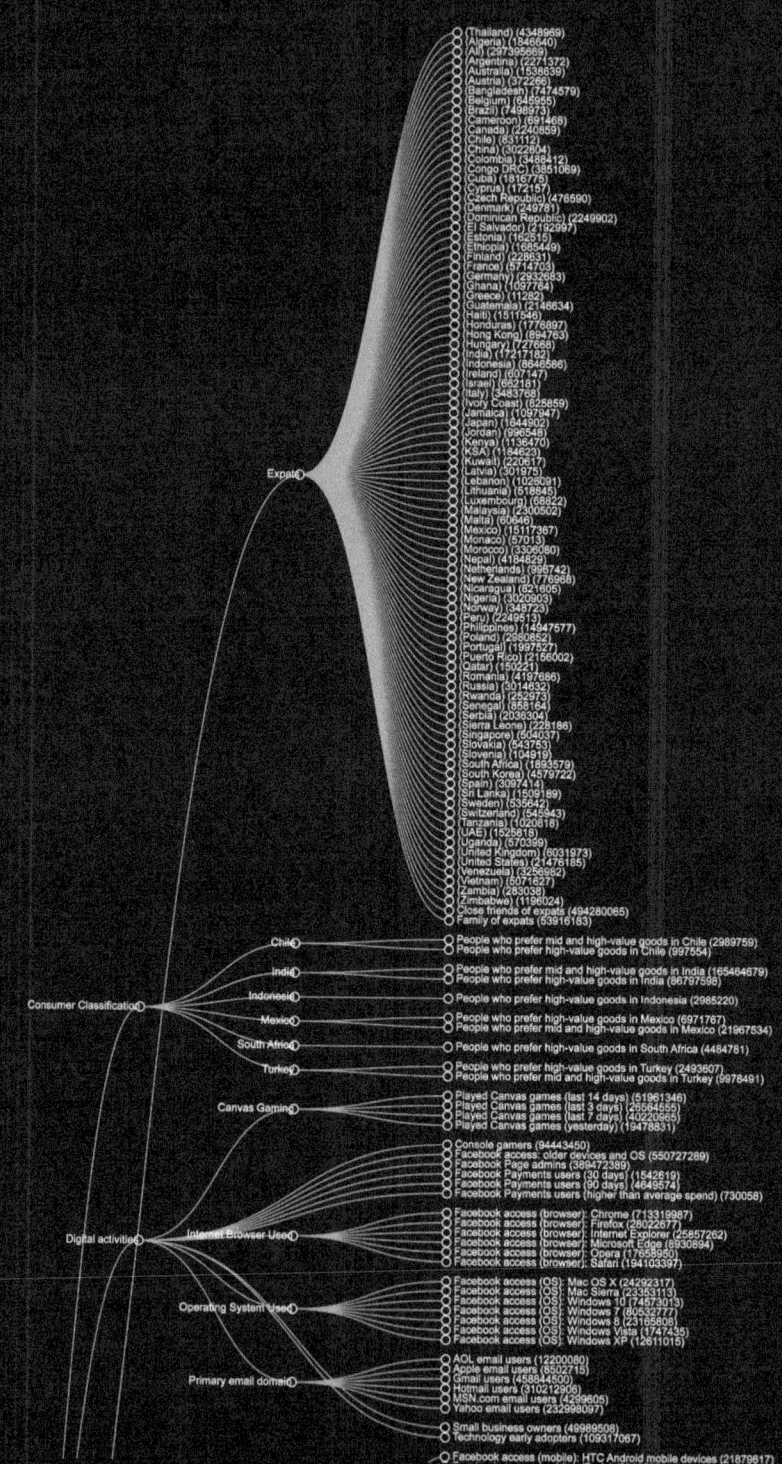

PROFILING THE PROFILERS
SOUSVEILLANCE OF BIG TECH COMPANIES USING THEIR OWN TOOLS

Based on state of the art big data analytics techniques, *Profiling The Profilers* is an artwork that generates a series of highly detailed digital profiles of Big Tech companies—ie. psychological, cultural and political profiles—similar to the ones constantly generated for each user by these very same companies. In other words, this algorithm performs a *sousveillance* of Big Tech companies using their own tools.

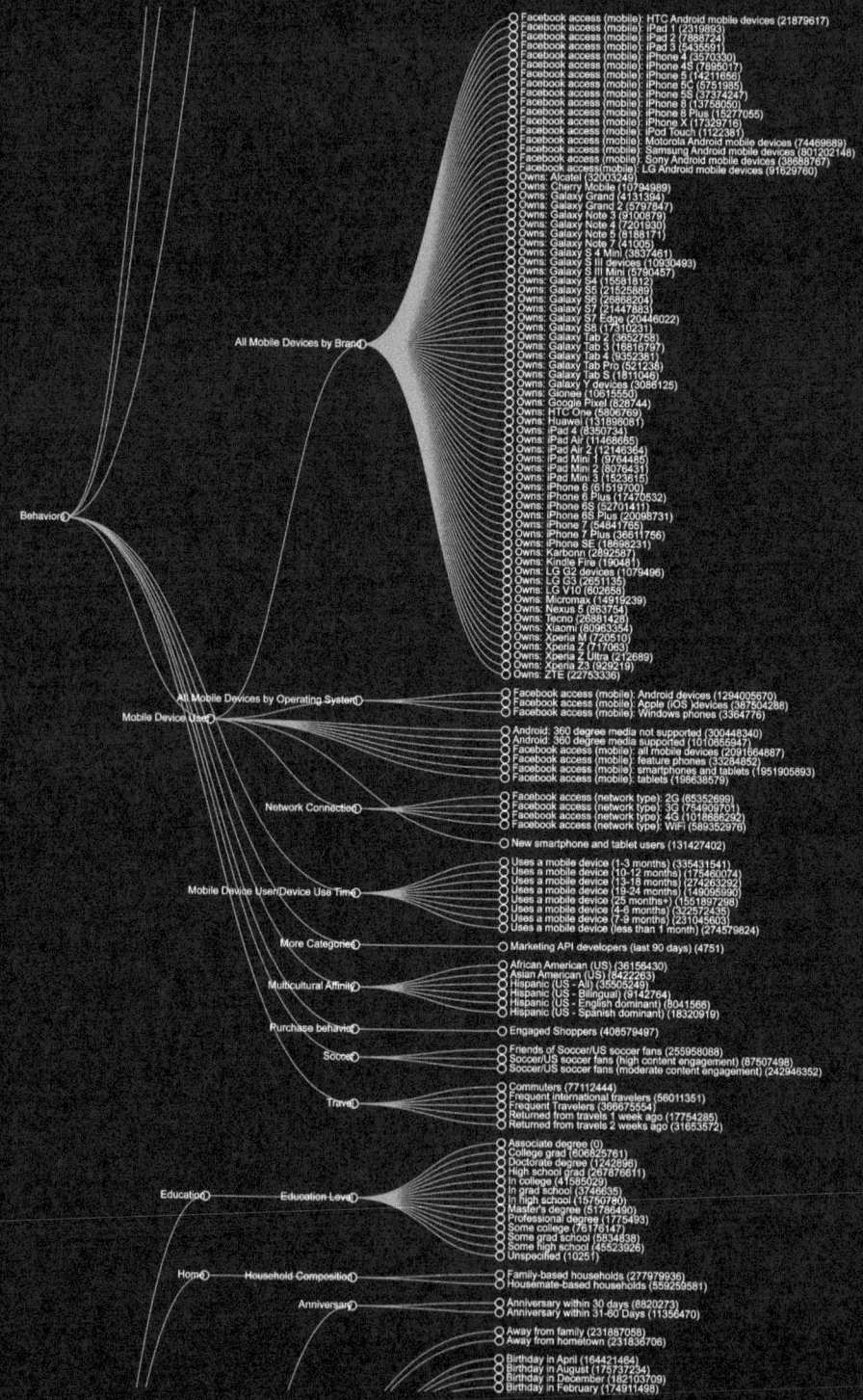

From Surveillance Capitalism to Glitch Capitalism

Today's Internet platforms are overly financed by advertisements. With 80% of global personal data which they offer to advertisers and third parties under unregulated policies, the major Big Tech companies (ie. Google, Amazon, Apple, Facebook and Microsoft) became pivotal actors in the shift towards the era of digital post-truth and the influence industry: micro-profiling, disinformation campaigns, bots, illegal data harvesting, troll farms, persuasive design.

This shift, contemporary to the emergence of the web 2.0, has been analyzed and problematized notably by Shoshana Zuboff. Surveillance capitalism is a "radically disembedded and extractive variant of information capitalism based on the commodification of 'reality' and its transformation into behavioral data for analysis and sales".

The extent of the process of automatization and surveillance is such, that our society has become an open laboratory for capitalist optimization. In April 2018, Malcolm Harris wrote about the concept of "glitch capitalism" for the *Intelligencer*. "The whole Silicon Valley ethos of 'move fast, break things' is essentially an endorsement of the glitch as a mode of production. America looks like a glitchy computer, and it's because capitalism is a machine language, reducible to numbers. America exists to create wealth, and the system isn't broken, it's just obeying the rules to disaster; as a country, we're more ourselves than ever".

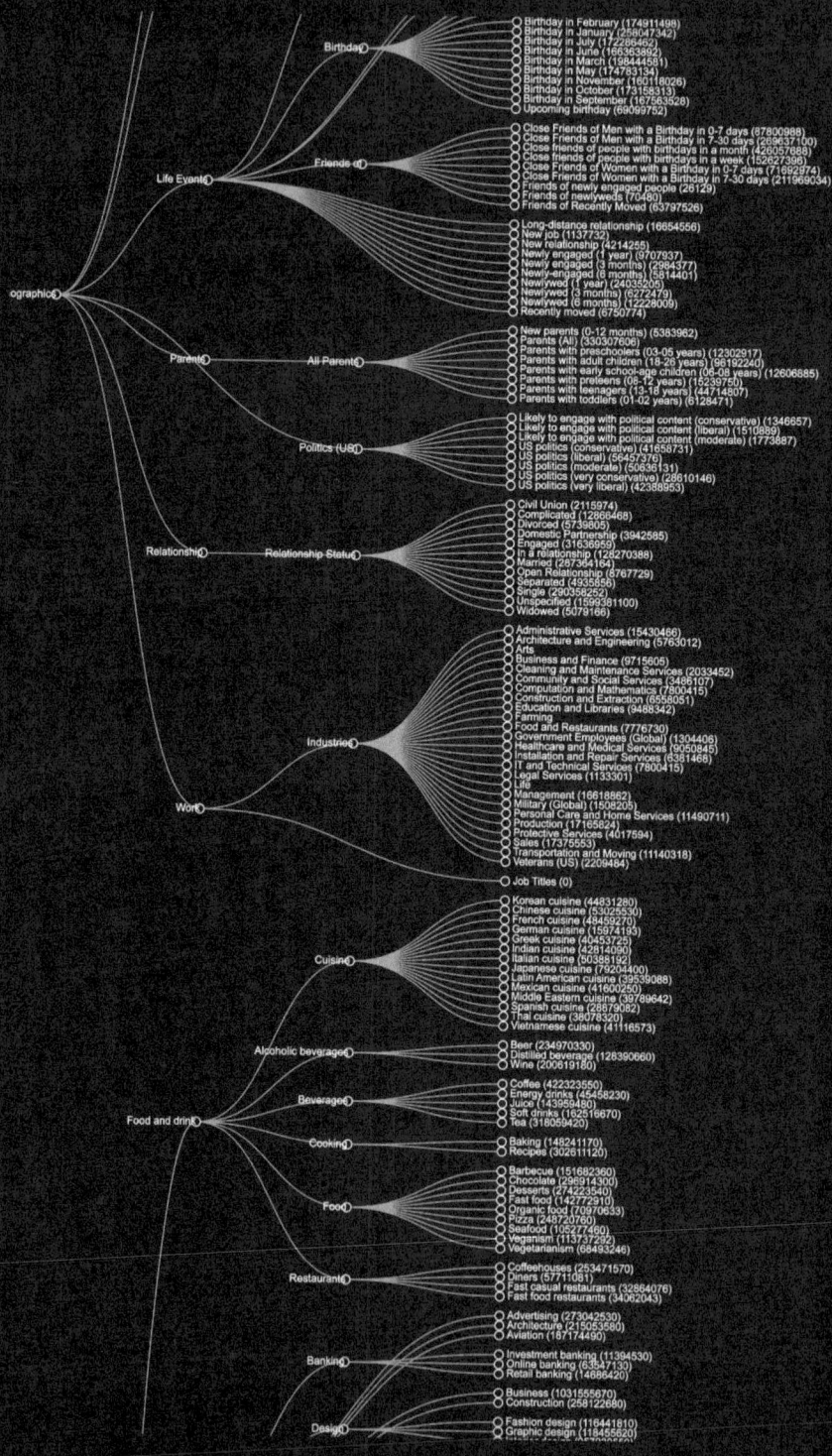

User Profiling

Digital profiling is the process of gathering and analyzing information about an individual that exists online. This is the use of algorithms or other mathematical techniques that allow the discovery of patterns or correlations in large quantities of data, aggregated in databases. A digital profile can include information about personal characteristics, behaviors, affiliations, connections and interactions.

Easily accessible digital records of behavior (ie. Facebook likes) can be used to automatically and quite accurately predict a range of highly sensitive personal attributes including: sexual orientation, ethnicity, religious and political views, personality traits, intelligence, happiness, use of addictive substances, parental separation, age, and gender.

The information environment has become the new modern battlefield where state and non-state actors employ sophisticated techniques for targeting, propaganda and disinformation (dark advertisements, nudging, algorithmic biases, social bots, sockpuppets, black propaganda, click farms...).

Interest

Business and industry

Design
- Graphic design (118455620)
- Interior design (257239550)

- Economics (118702860)
- Engineering (185155950)
- Entrepreneurship (193741640)
- Health care (158785030)
- Higher education (411503730)
- Management (203520550)
- Marketing (401564360)
- Nursing (111713610)

Online
- Digital marketing (40155120)
- Display advertising (1672190)
- Email marketing (5347700)
- Online advertising (52191310)
- Search engine optimization (14795770)
- Social media (284961400)
- Social media marketing (10645800)
- Web design (2162320)
- Web development (10988340)
- Web hosting (10243940)

Personal finance
- Credit cards (354109200)
- Insurance (210700320)
- Investment (222835610)
- Mortgage loans (87932410)

- Real estate (230876530)
- Retail (302713470)
- Sales (750644760)
- Science (344196950)
- Small business (47422860)
- Agriculture (220542910)

Entertainment

Games
- Action games (117802150)
- Board games (34088330)
- Browser games (19596180)
- Card games (83518900)
- Casino games (123334020)
- First-person shooter games (288338680)
- Gambling (319101220)
- Massively multiplayer online games (27877000)
- Massively multiplayer online role-playing games (47972923)
- Online games (212933160)
- Online poker (48151730)
- Puzzle video games (128417920)
- Racing games (56013470)
- Role-playing games (45615490)
- Shooter games (4737240)
- Simulation games (37502170)
- Sports games (61307050)
- Strategy games (2509460)
- Video games (891047740)
- Word games (37640780)

Live events
- Ballet (55140187)
- Bars (194645930)
- Concerts (234793980)
- Dancehalls (34512308)
- Music festivals (108617600)
- Nightclubs (205810230)
- Parties (238113320)
- Plays (215933320)
- Theatre (286082270)

Movies
- Action movies (238997950)
- Animated movies (176213960)
- Anime movies (162428612)
- Bollywood movies (224053510)
- Comedy movies (345893880)
- Documentary movies (129639670)
- Drama movies (162698530)
- Fantasy movies (148765600)
- Horror movies (150071470)
- Musical theatre (6882040)
- Science fiction movies (99526341)
- Thriller movies (173051180)

Music
- Blues music (157306130)
- Classical music (115406710)
- Country music (140718290)
- Dance music (141241170)
- Electronic music (285004190)
- Gospel music (116939430)
- Heavy metal music (168733530)
- Hip hop music (349152290)
- Jazz music (141057630)
- Music videos (530859690)
- Pop music (494032530)
- Rhythm and blues music (228538290)
- Rock music (501476320)
- Soul music (261307760)

Reading
- Books (5698847770)
- Comics (120985591)
- E-books (151586020)
- Fiction books (108254740)
- Literature (158909130)
- Magazines (287549460)
- Manga (92322471)
- Mystery fiction (96063550)
- Newspapers (52767560)
- Non-fiction books (13940495)
- Romance novels (61260103)

TV
- TV comedies (31196810)
- TV game shows (102177840)
- TV reality shows (195701270)
- TV talkshows (63395430)

Family and relationships
- Dating (208146030)
- Family (1073252060)
- Fatherhood (272536730)
- Friendship (96541750)
- Marriage (183863590)
- Motherhood (510120020)
- Parenting (109247189)
- Weddings (235598280)

Fitness and wellness
- Bodybuilding (119293914)
- Dieting (62577139)
- Gyms (238598653)
- Meditation (111029715)
- Nutrition (26692090)
- Physical exercise (358738510)
- Physical fitness (308412660)
- Running (132039775)
- Weight training (19828836)
- Yoga (182311436)
- Zumba (77334244)

Arts and music
- Acting (106613230)
- Crafts (92680810)
- Dance (557736550)
- Drawing (101731659)
- Drums (65120230)
- Fine art (38872302)
- Guitar (68026456)
- Painting (249587370)
- Performing arts (195104290)
- Photography (589550330)
- Sculpture (74713440)
- Singing (306897220)
- Writing (203934620)

- Current events (509327980)

Counter Profiling

As a response to this information asymmetry, we seized the means of data analytics to create a series of psychological, cultural and political profiles of the most data-extractivist Big Tech companies of our time: GAFAM, NATU, BATX, and others.

To do so, we worked for a year with dr. José Lages and his research team from Institut UTINAM, Besançon, France. In order to "infer hidden causal relations" between Big Tech companies and specific societal and political issues, we are using an algorithmic method derived from PageRank (reduced Google matrix analysis) to analyse the matrix of every possible link between every single Wikipedia article.

Similar algorithmic methods are often used in data science, data journalism, and for probabilistic user profiling. It allows to estimate the strength of the hidden relations between various members (articles, pages, users) of the studied network (for instance between a user and an item for the purpose of product recommendation).

These automated actions result in a series of highly detailed, and biased, digital profiles of big tech, similar to the ones constantly generated for each user by these very same companies.

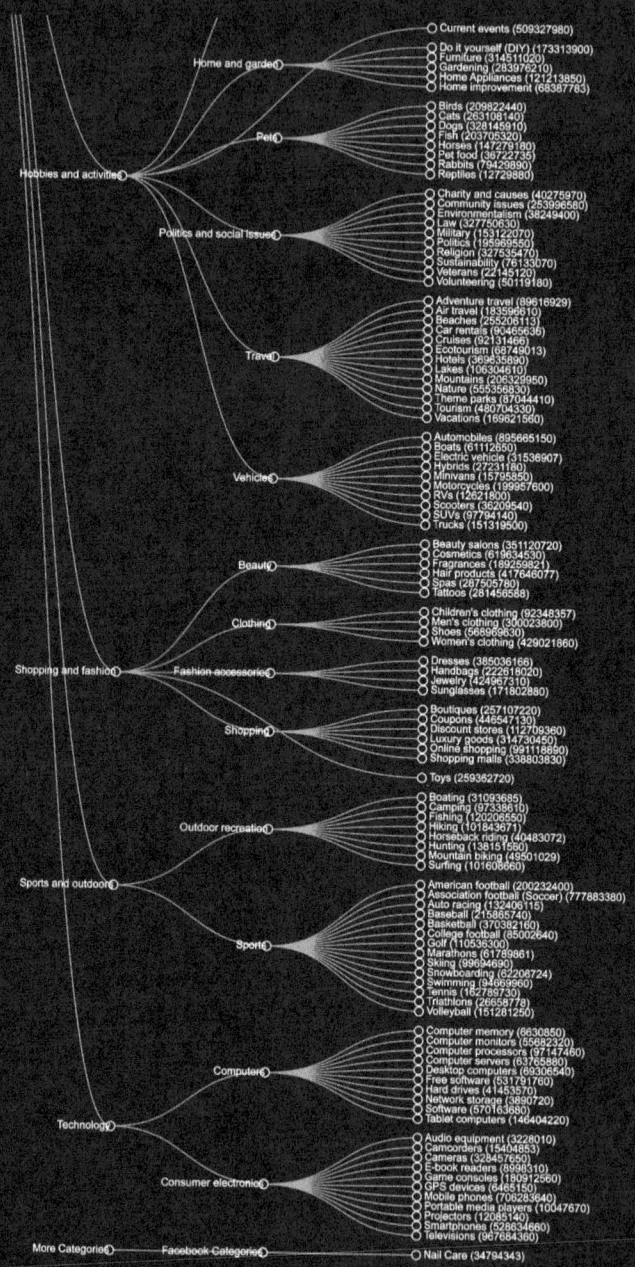

Facebook ads categories (USA 2018).

Targeting Big Tech Companies
GAFAM (Google, Apple, Facebook, Amazon, Microsoft)
NATU (Netflix, Airbnb, Tesla, Uber)
BATX (Baidu, Alibaba, Tencent, Xiaomi)

Rather than simply following the same categories as the ones usually tracked for the profiling and prediction of users' activity (age group, demographic, consumer behaviour, location, income group, etc.), we augmented these categories with additional critical insights, specifically relevant for Big Tech (political orientation, ethical orientation, propaganda techniques, type of induced addictions, types of biases, etc.).

This counter-profiling data will be continuously released on a dedicated platform as notifications, optimized for social media sharing by each visitor. This will result in a distributed counter-propaganda campaign, eventually polluting the social feeds of Big Tech companies.

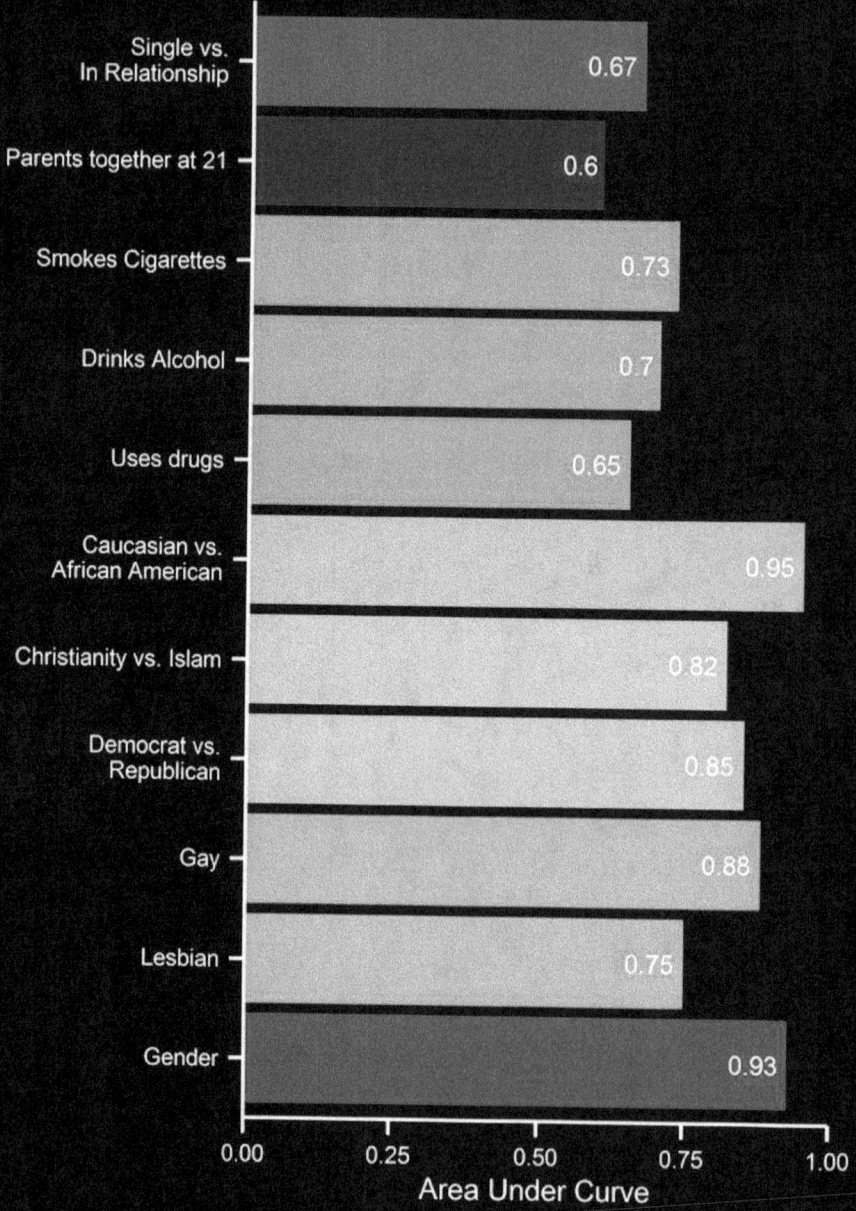

Private traits and attributes are predictable from digital records of human behavior, Michal Kosinski, David Stillwell, and Thore Graepel. Edited by Kenneth Wachter, University of California, Berkeley, CA, and approved Feb. 12, 2013 (received for review Oct. 29, 2012).

NOTES

Selection of scientific studies that applied Google matrix to datamine in various fields:

1   Capturing the influence of geopolitical ties from Wikipedia with reduced Google matrix [paper], Samer el Zant, Katia Jaffres-runser, Dima L. Shepelyansky.

2   Inferring hidden causal relations between pathway members using reduced Google matrix of directed biological networks [paper], José Lages, Dima L. Shepelyansky, Andrei Zinovyev.

3   Interactions of cultures and top people of Wikipedia from ranking of 24 language editions [paper], Young-ho Eom, Pablo Aragón, David Laniado, Andreas Kaltenbrunner, Sebastiano Vigna, Dima L. Shepelyansky.

PROFILING THE PROFILERS

2
PROFILING THE PROFILERS

EXCESSIVE BIG-DATA MINING AS A RIPOSTE STRATEGY

ALESSANDRO LUDOVICO

NETFLIX vs NEW RELIGIOUS MOVEMENTS

PROFILING THE PROFILERS
(EXCESSIVE BIG-DATA MINING
AS A RIPOSTE STRATEGY)

What should be the role of art in the current tyrannical ecology of online information, dominated globally by a handful of Big Tech corporations who possess 80% of our online personal data [1]? If we can find clues in the less complex previous decades, then it should not be too hard to find examples in contemporary art of dissecting and reformulating the "power," breaking its inaccessible overarching aura, and formulating strategies to de-escalate it to the mundane level and, in doing so, in some way annihilating its own ruling demeanour.

In the last few years, DISNOVATION.ORG have questioned the hegemonic ecologies of information at different levels throughout their own artistic practice. They have ironically researched and explored the technical edges of monopolistic AI in *Predictive Art Bot*, a bot using headlines to predict art concepts. Similarly they have engaged in the flourishing and unstoppable underground of infinite copying in *The Pirate Cinema*, a real-time visualisation of the continuously exchanged movie files. Their latest articulation of a conceptual information resistance is *The Web Politics Trilogy*, a trilogy of artworks systematically addressing key aspects of our information ecology.

In the first artwork *The Persuadables*, a minimal glossary of strategies used to effectively manipulate opinions online on any scale is compiled and illustrated. It takes the form of a video, fully opening the Pandora's vase of these manipulative techniques, thereby exposing how they accomplish their goals. It is a frightening and accurate explanation, in the tradition of disenchanted avant-garde and counter-cultural debunking systems of power. And it poses a critical systemic issue, still largely unanswered at legal, political and cultural levels.

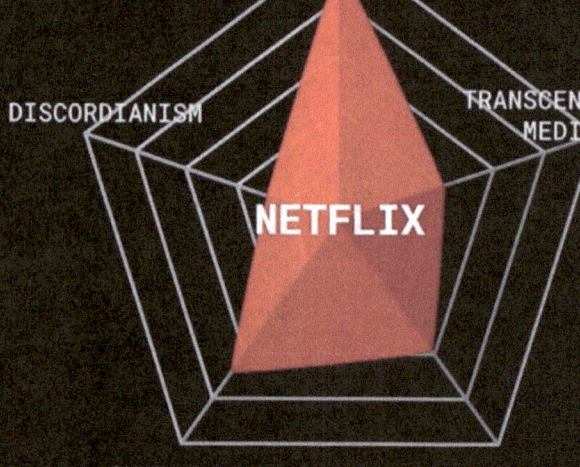

The second artwork in the trilogy is the *Online Culture Wars* map, produced in various formats, including a freely downloadable PDF or printed as a classic stack of take-away touristic maps. It provides an iconographic synthesis of controversial online symbols and agents in a compact form. It positions the most popular visual elements of online "wars" as universal triggers in the form of shared codes and symbols, feeding instant online political frictions. If Josh On's *We Rule* [2] painstakingly compiled his own datasets, rendering them as a dynamic, explorable picture of the American ruling elite in the early 2000s, this work agglomerates the self-empowered signifiers of online debates' hyper-inflated world, expressing a similarly disturbing concentration of power and influence.

After *The Persuadables*, that compiled the essential list of concepts in order to fully comprehend the ecological information crisis, the *Online Culture Wars* map provides the compass to orientate us through its visual assault. They complement each other in understanding the same scattered but solid conceptual structure of dominance, thereby contributing to develop a critical awareness and acting as discussion starters. Both intrinsically are instrumental in reversing the online power games, or the consolidated relationships reinforced by the distributed and disguised online propaganda.

As a follow up to these two strategic tools (a comprehensive map and a revealing glossary), the last part of the trilogy *Profiling the Profilers* presents a symbolic action to re-appropriate the lost space of direct dialogue with the infrastructure's owners.

Profiling the Profilers is DISNOVATION.ORG's counter narrative to data extractivism. It is based on an app created with scientific support of the Institut UTINAM in France, specialised in big data analytics techniques. In this work, public datasets and machine learning approaches have been used to create "psychological, cultural and political" profiles of Big Tech companies like Apple, Facebook, Google, Amazon, Microsoft and many others. The

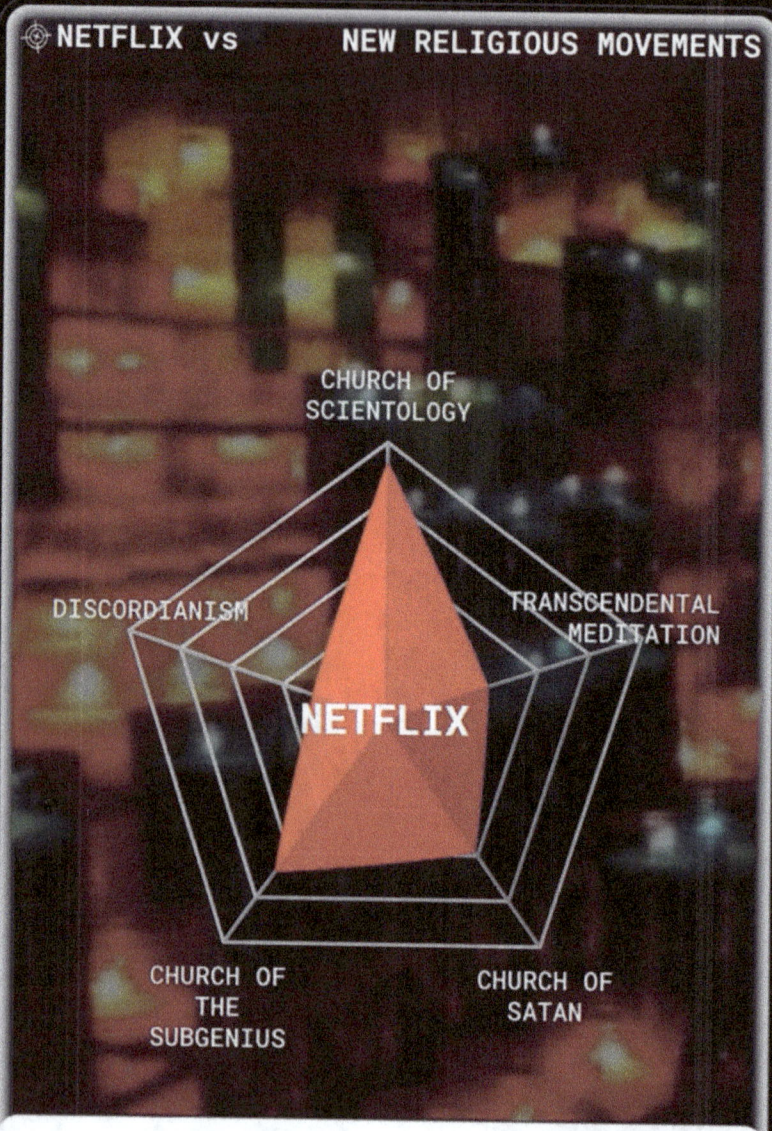

process involves a deep data analysis conducted in the same fashion the targeted companies are conducting their activities to profile their customers. The duo have then developed a bot that discovers and extracts meaning from the hidden links among different datasets related to these companies, quantifying their association and embodiment of specific values. They have structured this action in order to "infer hidden causal relations" between Big Tech companies and specific societal and political issues [3]. The relevant discoveries of the profiling process are shared as notifications to a mass of users who can then disseminate them on the official social media channels of the companies, collectively exposing them in a new more comprehensive fashion.

Within the visual interface of this app, the consistency of the results being calculated live and animated is highly shareable on social media. Its aesthetics conceptually render the algorithms subsequently, and the political statement in the computed associations is sublimated in the invitation to share it right away on social media. It is a minimal time required for the active calculation of possible meaning, which then translates into potential action shortly afterwards. The user is accompanied through a fast, new and challenging interrelation up to the point of advocating it.

In its installation form, the smartphone screen is scaled up to the size of a digital billboard ("targeting the Big-Tech, instead of common users" in the artists' words), shrink-wrapped together with boxes on a standard Euro-pallet (a "representation of the physicality of the industrial"). Here, the physical presence of a delivery is symbolically functional of the "upstream" tech corporations' need, and it couples with the downstream induced by the use of these platforms (the ad hoc advertisement, the notifications, the e-commerce, etc.). The installation is embodied both in its sculptural form and in the impalpable form of the process flowing (from calculation to social media post). It becomes a nearly monumental representation of the parallel mass-scale

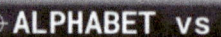

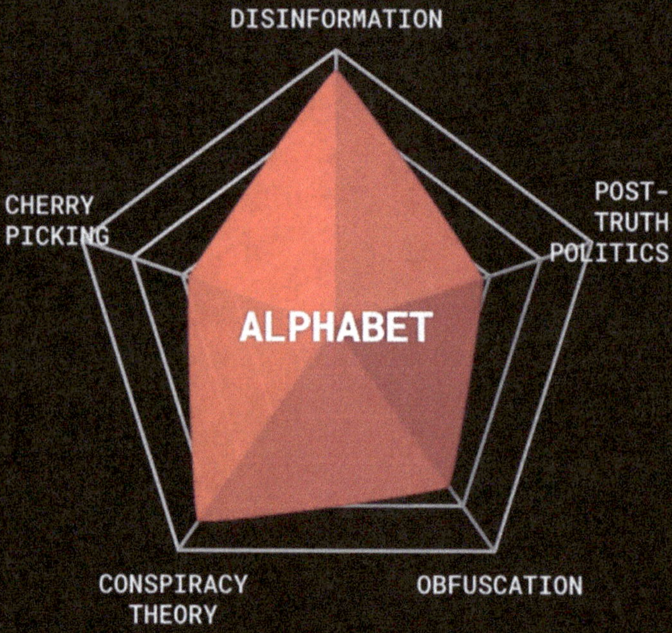

global operations exchange: the capital delivering its goods through globalised shipping, and the data economy computing its results and pervading the social media.

The companies involved in this work are perceived as shiny and huge impenetrable entities, which will be then "profiled back" for what they truly are: enormous media infrastructures of influential content and socio-political disruption, not just mere IT giants, as usually perceived by common sense. In this respect DISNOVATION.ORG is applying Greg Elmer's definition: "to profile is to attempt to account for the unknown—our inability to adequately capture, contain, or regulate and govern behaviour, thought, language, and action." [4] Their "unknown," here, starts to be unveiled, and it relates directly to both classic profiling techniques and investigative journalism.

But as art historian Antonia Majaca mentioned during a public debate at the Venice Biennale [5], this is the time of a different AI, the "Artist's Intelligence," which should provide the criticism mostly lost in the algorithms, and the consequent original contribution to the collective elaboration of strategies. The artists are acting as a subversive short circuit, using the same oppressing infrastructure. Like Cildo Meireles, who in his *Ideological Circuits: Coca-Cola Project* altered and redistributed reusable Coca-Cola bottles in 1970, adding rebellious or philosophical content, which was mimicking the brand design in its inscriptions [6].

DISNOVATION.ORG equally intervenes in the guarded territories of communication with a political statement. On one hand, they prove how the propaganda of the Big Tech sector is disproportionately powerful: they cannot compete with the economic and legal armies of these companies. Yet they also hint at the scale of the bias which is polluting the algorithms, organising a symbolic counter-act. They are formulating and then "publishing" algorithmic inferences which are meant to be shared and possibly discussed. They will make a public call by launching the app,

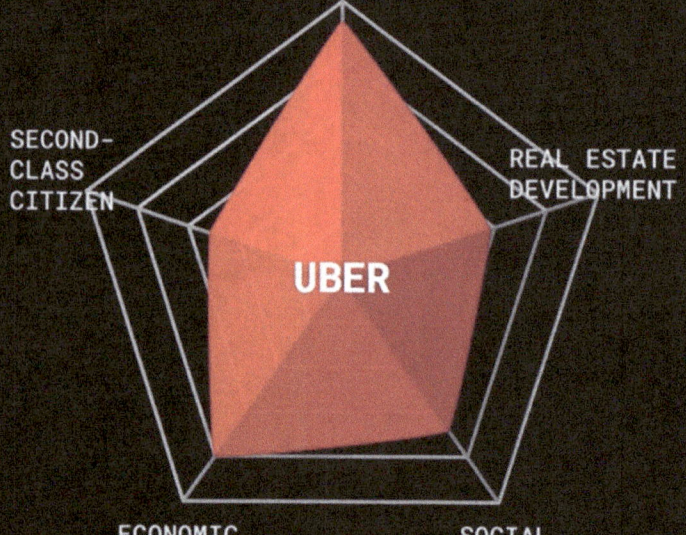

to send back the companies' propaganda info-toxins, creating conceptual antibodies, collectively metabolized. The single individual can have, then, an important role, contributing to counter-propaganda which is developed through humour and by adopting a Dada-like attitude. This almost desperate attempt to interact with these abstract giants (which are hard to locate and address physically) is a direct way of talking *back*. So, if current AI is mostly a vertical type of intelligence, hyper specialized in a narrow set of purposes and tasks, not dissimilar to what we often hear about academia, DISNOVATION.ORG's artist intelligence is acting and talking back and, in doing so, redefining the public image of these media giants through a collective debate, fuelled by inscrutable machines' calculations.

—Alessandro Ludovico

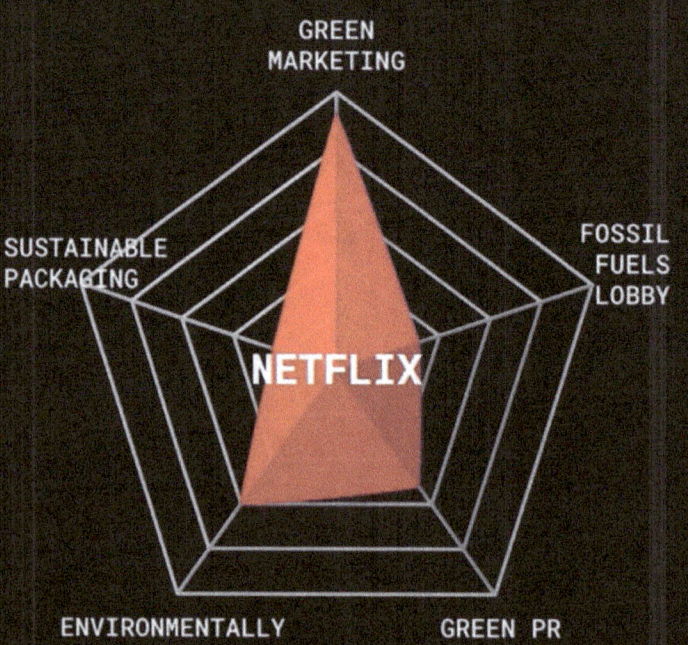

NOTES

1   Reportage by Canal+ "Big Data: les nouveaux devins" https://www.youtube.com/watch?v=5mmQeb8mXVk&feature=youtu.be

2   Josh On, We Rule, 2002, http://www.theyrule.net/2001/

3   Inga Seidler, Schloss-Post, Issue No 0 -"Digital Culture, Theory & Art, From Surveillance Capitalism to Glitch Capitalism, Interview with DISNOVATION.ORG"—Sep 05, 2019
https://schloss-post.com/from-surveillance-capitalism-to-glitch-capitalism/

4   Elmer, Greg. 2003. Profiling Machines Mapping the Personal Information Economy. The MIT Press. P. 134.

5   "58th Venice Biennale and Liechtenstein Brunch / Art in Dataspace symposium", Neural #64, Ass. Cult. Neural, 2019.

6   Cildo Meireles, Insertions into Ideological Circuits: Coca-Cola Project, 1970, https://www.tate.org.uk/research/publications/performance-at-tate/perspectives/cildo-meireles

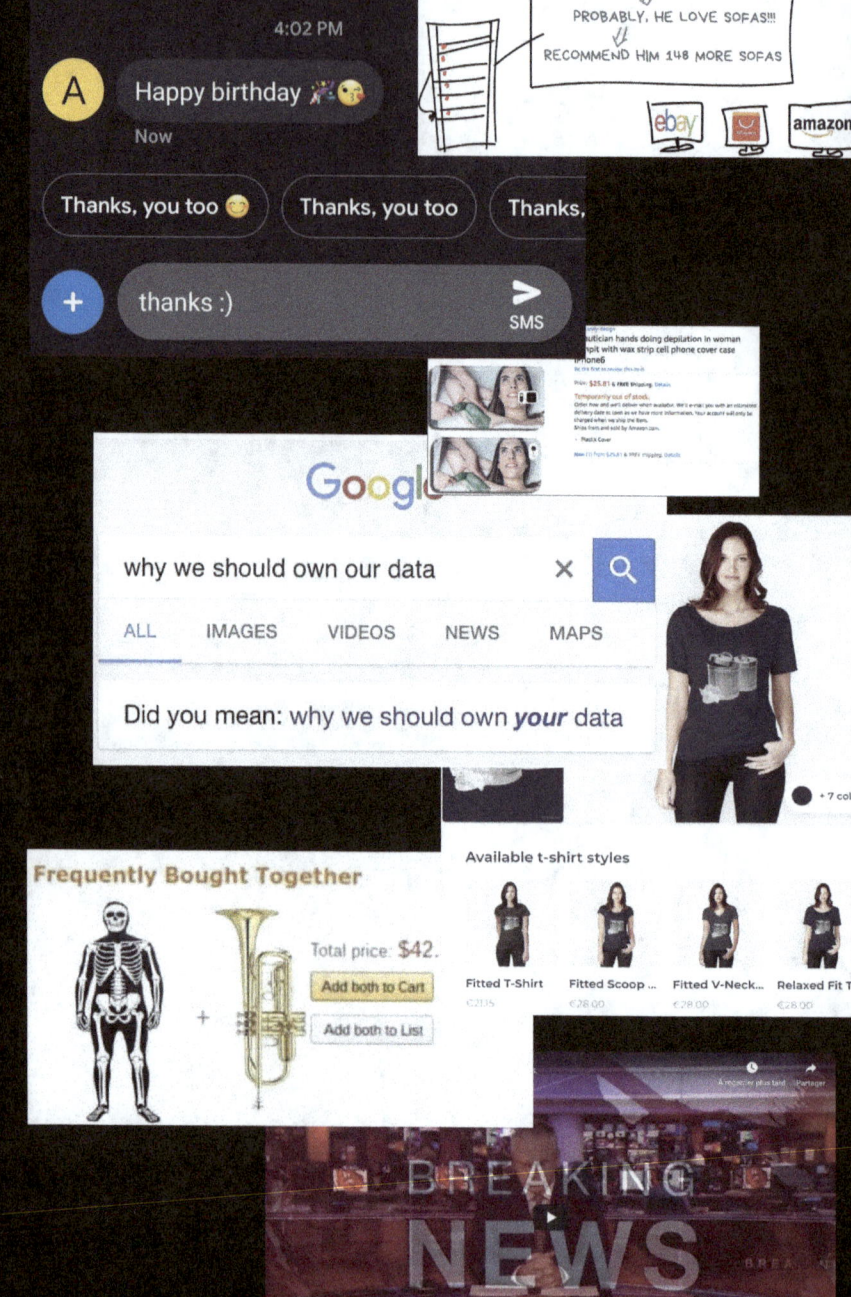

3
FROM SURVEILLANCE CAPITALISM TO GLITCH CAPITALISM

INTERVIEW BY INGA SEIDLER

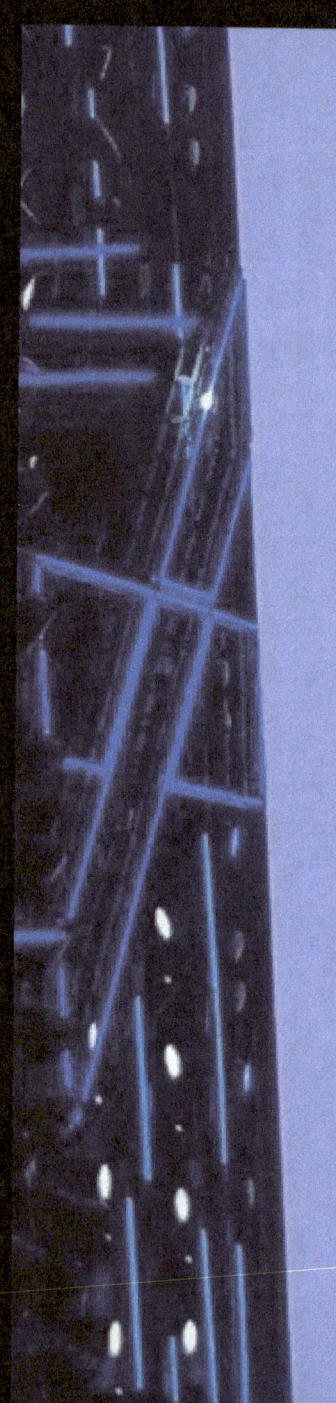
Day 1 of Qualtrics Keynote Sessions in Salt Lake City, Utah

FROM SURVEILLANCE CAPITALISM
TO GLITCH CAPITALISM

Inga Seidler: Your proposal says: *Profiling the Profilers* will result in a "series of highly detailed, and biased, digital profiles of Big Tech, similar to the ones constantly generated for each user by these very same companies, and then result in a distributed counter-propaganda campaign, eventually polluting the social feeds of Big Tech companies". Could you explain in more detail—what kind of information are you interested in with regards to GAFAM? What kind of data are you collecting? And how could these profiles look like?

DISNOVATION.ORG: With this new project, *Profiling the Profilers*, the first idea was to attempt a simple, but almost impossible action: reverse the surveillance of the Big Tech companies using their own tools & methods. To do so, we spent one year working with Dr. José Lages and his research team from Institut UTINAM, in Besançon. Based on state of the art big data analytics techniques, this work will generate a series of highly detailed digital profiles of Big Tech companies (ie. psychological, cultural and political profiles), similar to the ones constantly generated for each user by these very same companies.

To assemble these digital profiles, rather than simply follow the same categories as the ones usually tracked for the profiling and prediction of users' activity (age group, demographic, consumer behaviour, location, income group, etc.), we will augment these categories with additional critical insights, specifically relevant for Big Tech (political orientation, ethical orientation, propaganda techniques, type of induced addictions, types of biases, etc.).

In order to "infer hidden causal relations" between Big Tech companies and specific societal and political issues, we are using an algorithmic method derived from PageRank (reduced Google matrix analysis) in order to analyse the matrix of every possible link between every single existing Wikipedia article.

Wikipedia mining of hidden links between political leaders, Klaus Frahm, Katja Jaffres-Runser, Dima Shepelyansky, 2013

Similar algorithmic methods are often used in data sciences, data journalism, and for probabilistic user profiling. It allows to estimate the strength of the hidden relations between various members (articles, pages, users) of the studied network (for instance between a user and an item for the purpose of product recommendation).

IS: What can we expect from the project / the research material / preview of the project as you will publish it on Schlosspost, who created the materials and how?

D: The first release on Schlosspost will be focusing on our research material and the core elements of our work methodology. A few weeks later, we will release the interactive online project. The algorithm we used is based on the research of Dr. José Lages' team, and the programming is done with our long time collaborator Jerome Saint-Clair. Our article on Schlosspost will include academic references, articles, and visual elements, for instance on online persuasion, surveillance capitalism, or this fascinating article about glitch capitalism.

IS: What are the next steps / different formats the project will take on?

D: We're presently in a residency with M-Cult (Helsinki) and Emap to finalize this installation. We will release the online project this fall, and then the exhibition version in November 2019. The online project will also unfold over time, as users eventually take part in the sharing of the counter-propaganda developed by the "Profiling The Profilers" bot. As users will share or repost some of the generated counter-recommendations, these posts will end up polluting the feeds, and the hashtags of the targeted Big Tech companies.

The interview was conducted by Inga Seidler.

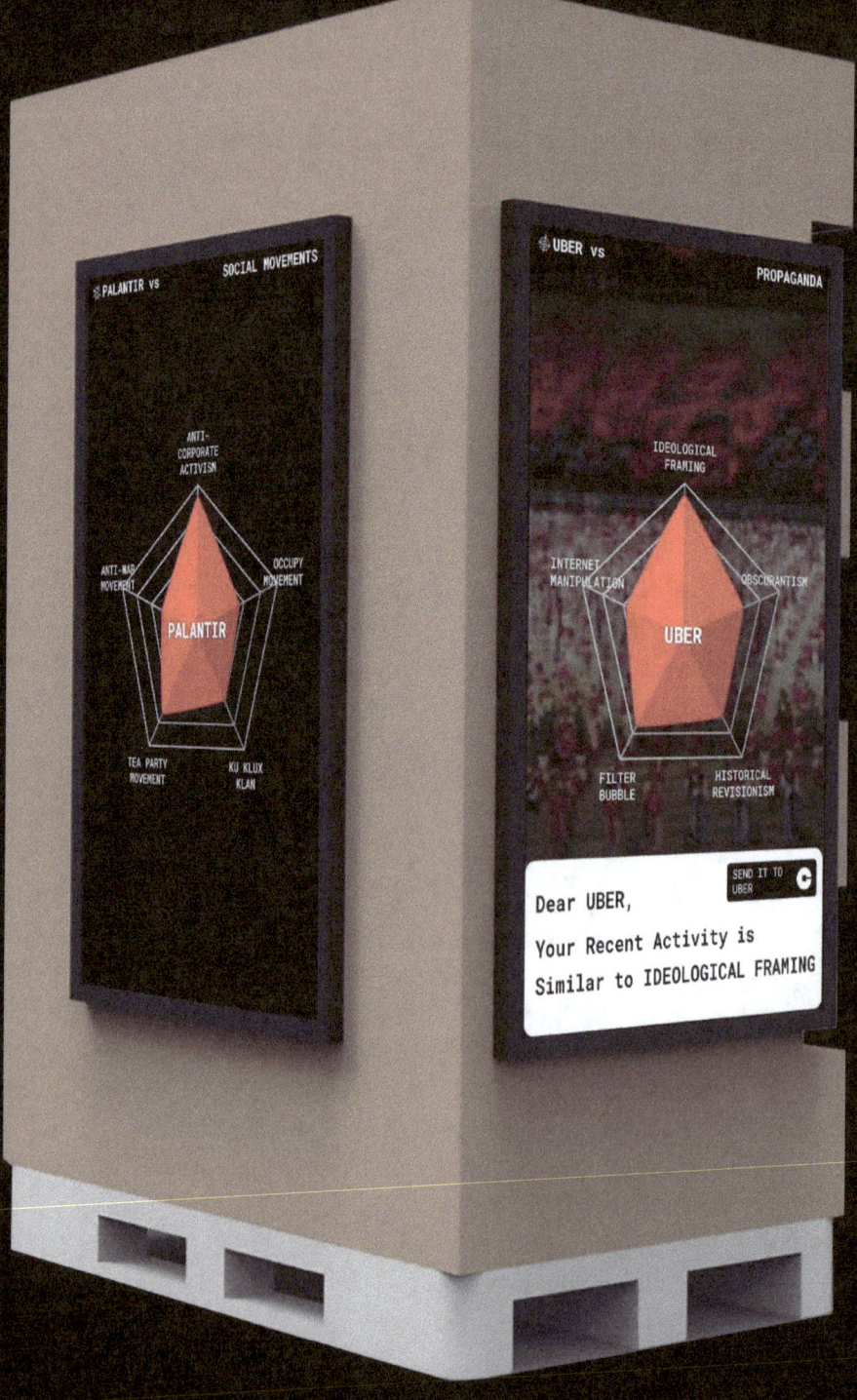

4
PROFILING THE PROFILERS

PROTOTYPES & EXHIBITION VIEWS

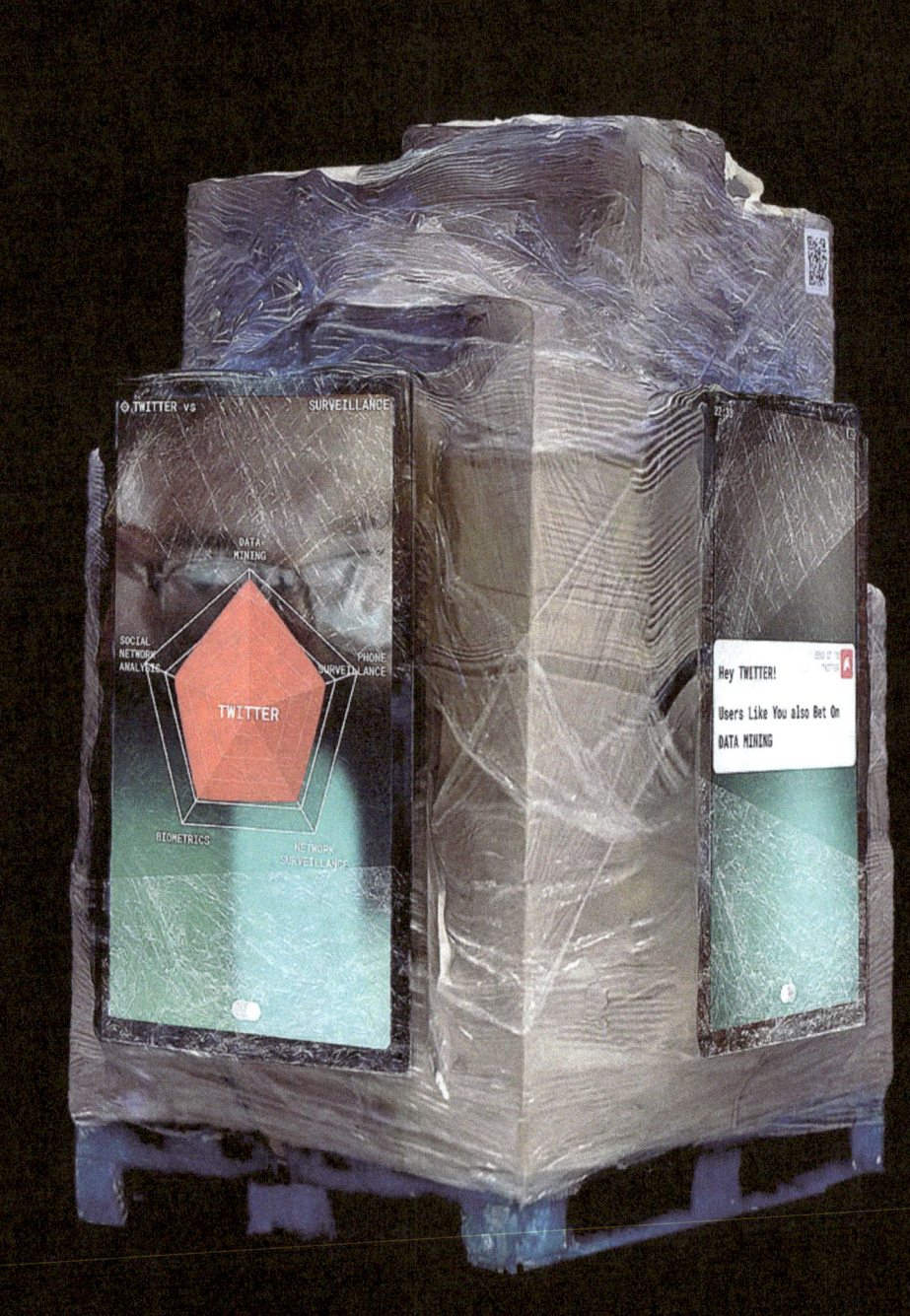

Profiling The Profilers (3D scan), La Gaîté Lyrique, Paris (2019).

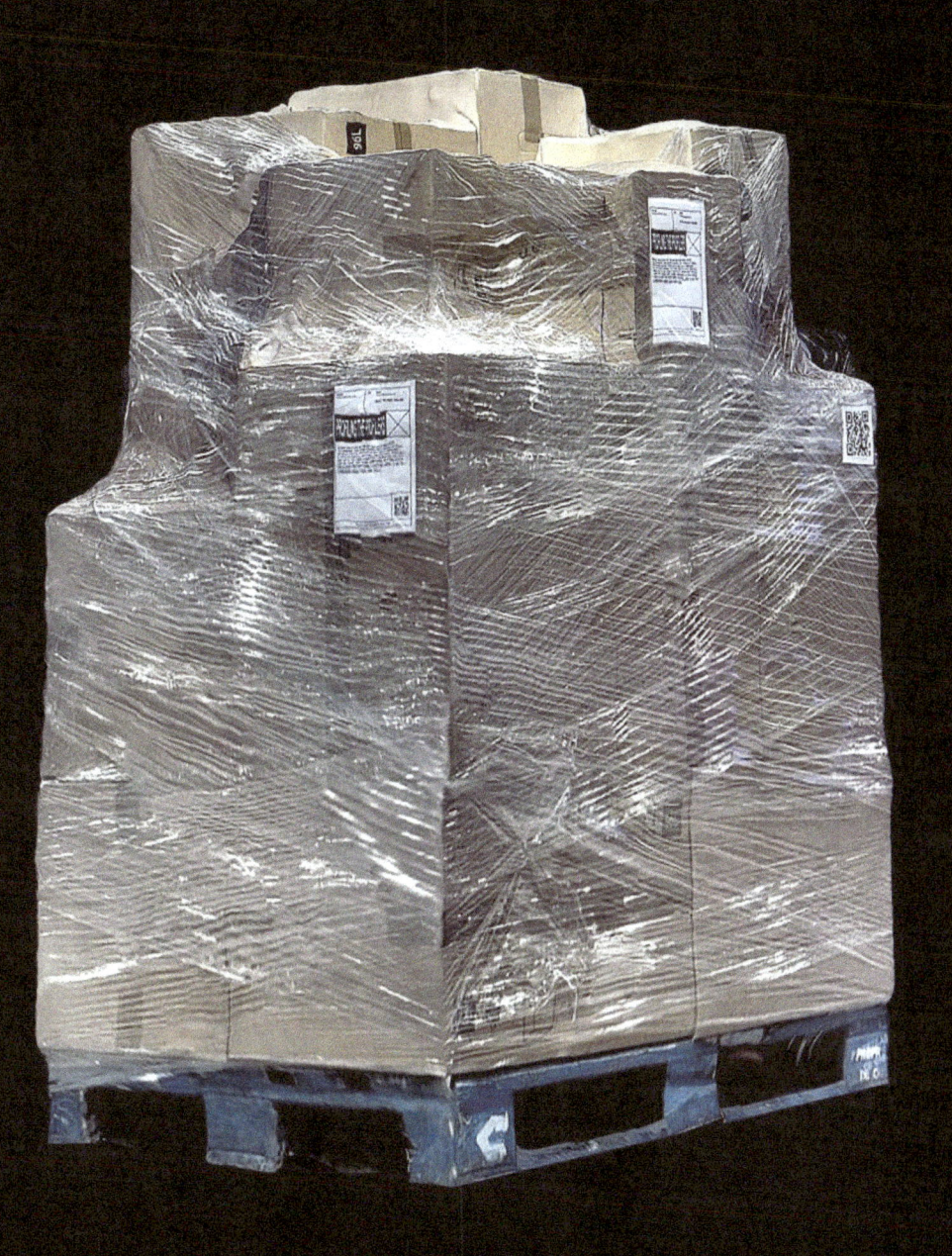

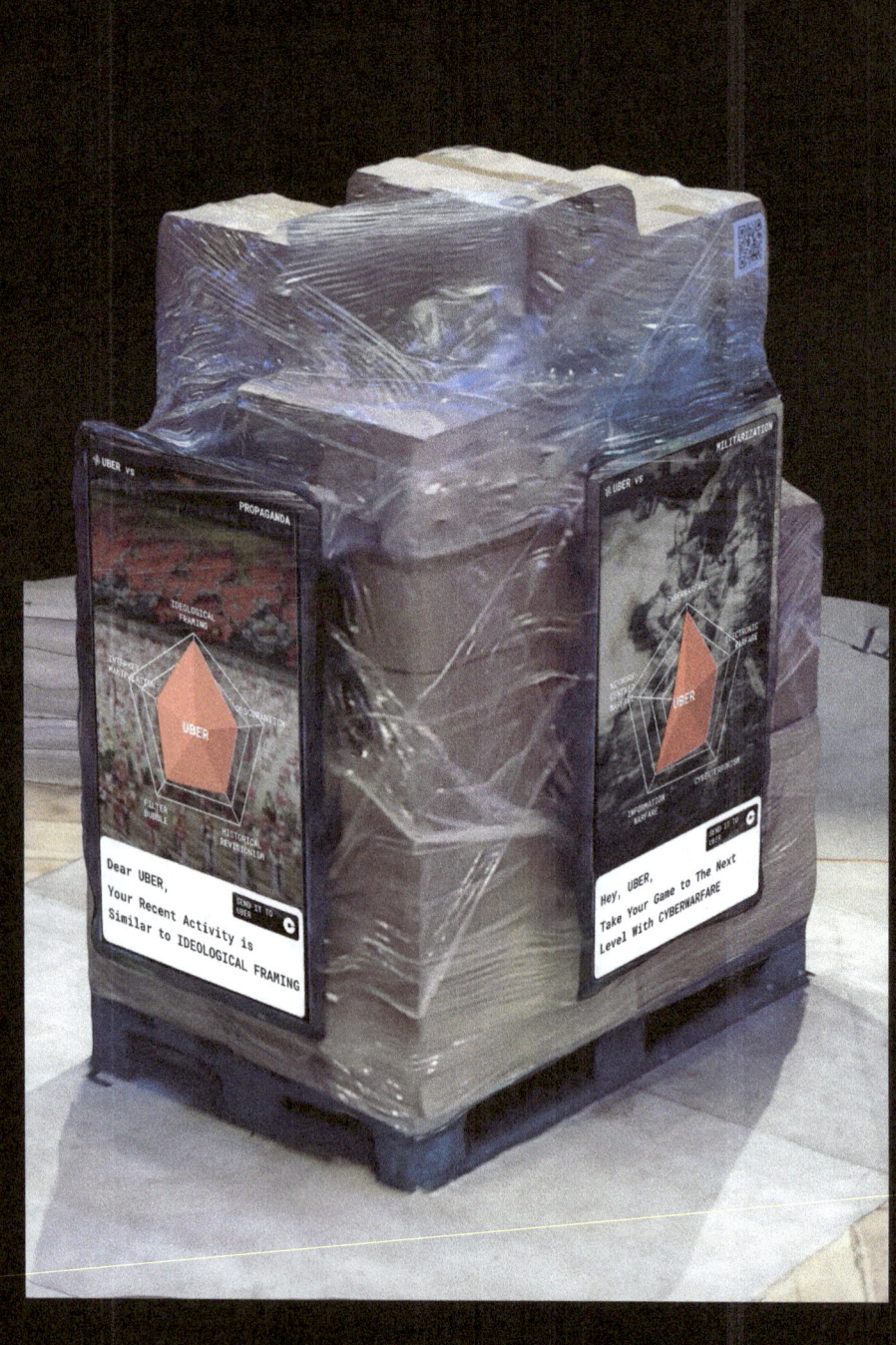

Profiling The Profilers (3D scan), La Gaîté Lyrique, Paris (2019).

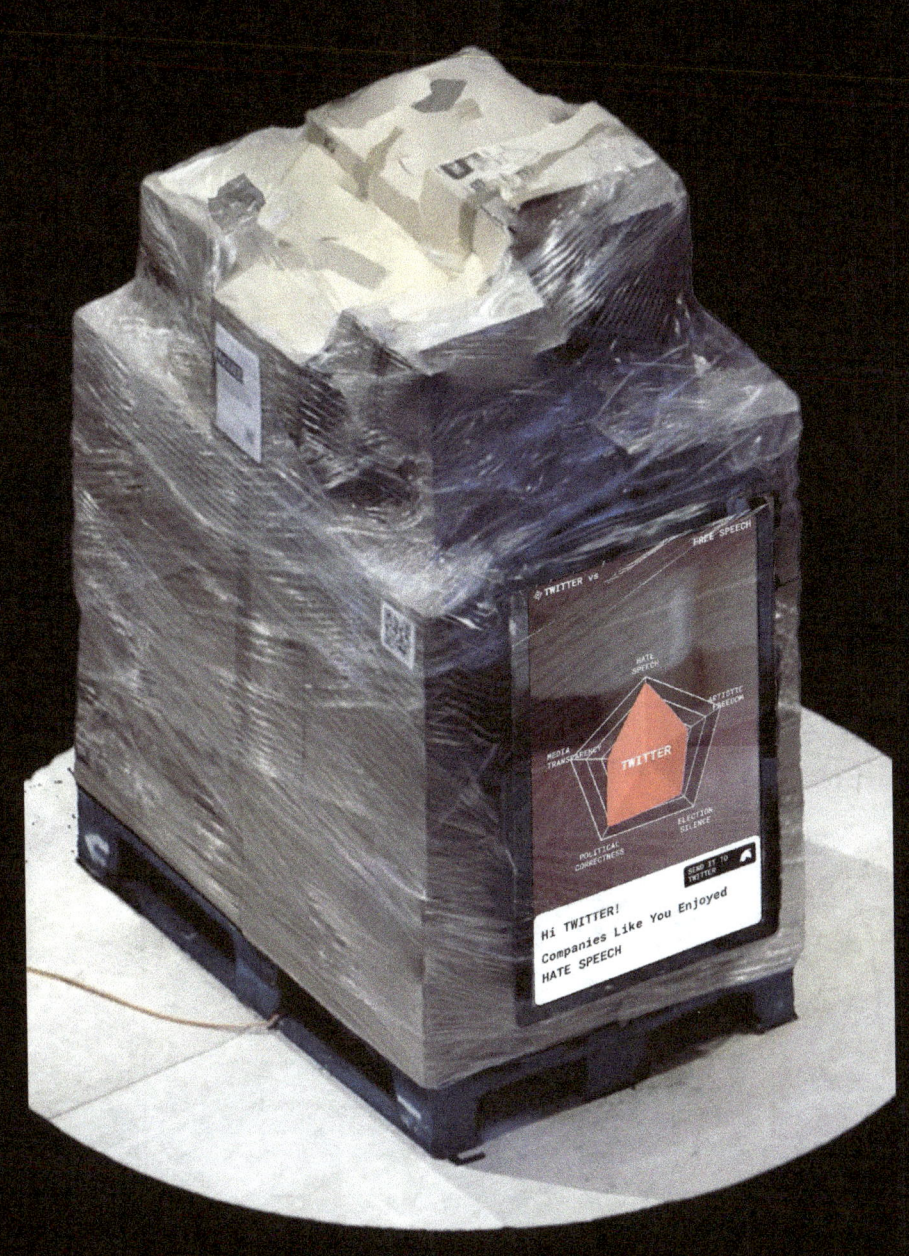

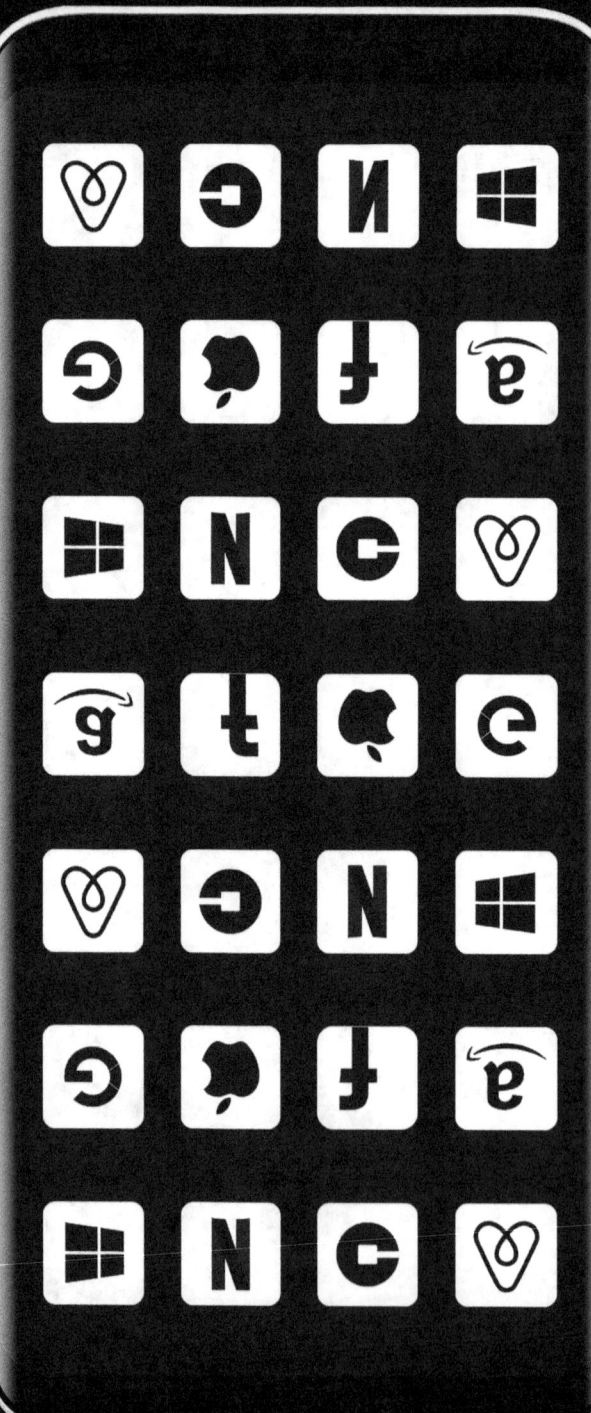

PROFILING THE PROFILERS (2018-2019)

profilingtheprofilers.com

A project by DISNOVATION.ORG (Nicolas Maigret & Maria Roszkowska)

Programming by Jerome Saint-Clair

Space design Lucie Gautrain

Graphic design Maria Roszkowska (DISNOVATION.ORG)

Translation Themba Bhebhe ("Profiling the Profilers, Excessive Big-Data Mining as a Riposte Strategy")

Scientific support of Dr. José Lages, Institut UTINAM, France

Supported by NRW-Forum Düsseldorf (DE), MU artspace Eindhoven (NL), Institut UTINAM Besançon (FR) (with José Lages), M-Cult (FI) (with EMAP/EMARE, Creative Europe), La Gaîté Lyrique (FR).

The Work was realised within the framework of the European Media Art Platforms EMARE program at m-cult with support of the Creative Europe Culture Programme of the European Union.

Many thanks to Minna Tarkka, José Lages, Alessandro Ludovico, Marie Lechner & Inga Seidler.

Exhibited at:
V2: Launch @ HASH Awards, ZKM, Karlruhe, 2020 [DE]
V1: Festival accès)s(#20, Pau, 2020 [FR]
V1: BIO26 the Design Biennial, Ljubljana, 2020 [SLO]
V1: Network Effects, Oodi, Helsinki, 2019 [FI]
V0: MUTEK-SF, San Francisco, 2019 [USA]
V0: Institut UTINAM, CNRS, Besançon, 2018 [FR]
V0: The New Newsroom, MU Artspace, Eindhoven, 2018 [NL]
V0: Im Zweifel für den Zweifel, NRW-Forum, Düsseldorf, 2018 [DE]

www.ingramcontent.com/pod-product-compliance
Lightning Source LLC
Chambersburg PA
CBHW070839220526
45466CB00002B/826